Dear Diva

A comedy

Jan Harris

Samuel French—London
www.samuelfrench-london.co.uk

FOR AMATEUR PRODUCTION ENQUIRIES

UNITED KINGDOM AND WORLD
EXCLUDING NORTH AMERICA
plays@samuelfrench.co.uk
020 7255 4302/01

Each title is subject to availability from Samuel French,
depending upon country of performance.

DEAR DIVA

First performed at RADA's John Gielgud Theatre on 8th August 2011 with the following cast of characters:

Frances	Janice Day
Taxi Driver	Andrew Ward
Ezzlie	Jenny Logan

Directed by Matthew Gould

CHARACTERS

Frances
Taxi Driver
Ezzlie

The action takes place in Frances' sitting-room, in the village of Little Mansion, near Carlisle

Time—the present

DEAR DIVA

SCENE 1

A shabby but tidy sitting-room

Frances, a middle age woman dowdily dressed, is plumping up the pink cushions on the sofa. She looks out of the window expectantly, and for something to do picks up her diary

Frances Dear Diary, It's a long time since I logged anything with you, and that's simply because nothing much happened after the funeral. But today, today! I have lots to tell you. I have been sworn to secrecy but I shall burst if I can't talk about it. She's coming! She's coming here! Her agent called me and thanked me for my letter; he didn't refer to all the other letters I had written, just to the one where I said there is room in my home for her. I even quoted she could "Come Rat-Tat-Tat-Ting on My Front Door Any Day or Night". That was one of her early hits, but I don't think he remembered. I have to keep pinching myself, because, She-is-coming-here! I got the idea when I saw her on the telly. She hadn't been at all well, a shadow of her old self. Seems, since she left Hollywood, she has been living in hotels and now they want their money, or her money, but she hasn't got any. They're suing her for thousands! They should be honoured to have such a big star in their midst! Those London hotels know how to charge; I stayed in one once, the coat hanger was chained to the cupboard, and a distinct smell of urine coming from the sink in the room. But that's another story! The agent seemed quite keen on the idea, said he would see to it personally that she would be on the train to Carlisle;

I kept telling him that Little Mansion was our village near Carlisle, but he wasn't much of a listener, just kept on saying this was to be our secret. How do you keep someone like her a secret? Can you keep the Eiffel Tower a secret? Or the Empire State Building, or the Tower of London a secret? The woman is a legend; she's filled our lives for years! Well, my life ... She's filled my little life ... I'll give her the big room, Mam's room, and I'll move to the little room again. I know pink is her favourite colour, and Earl Grey is her favourite tea, strange that for an American. I've stocked up on pink toilet rolls, and pink scented-soap for the bathroom, I hope she won't mind sharing the bathroom with me. So, there I've said it. Ezzlie Harlow star of stage, screen and radio is coming here. Here into my village, into my house, into my life ... I did it! The first time in my life I've made something happen; not some little everyday thing, not just a trip to the city and back, oh no! I've turned fantasy into reality, because Ezzlie Harlow is going to be my friend ——

The doorbell rings. Frances snaps closed her diary and rushes to open the door

A Taxi Driver slams a heavy suitcase down and starts ranting in a heavy eastern european accent

Taxi Driver Misses! I have mad woman out here in my taxi. She saying I hijack her. But this is the address she gives me. Twenty-two, End Road, Little Mansion. She's refuse to pay me!
Frances Oh my God! It's her! She's come! (*She waves toward the cab*)
Taxi Driver I'm not going till I have money!
Frances She's coming! Make way!

Ezzlie sweeps in

Ezzlie (*in a booming voice*) Do you have a telephone?
Frances (*curtsying*) This way.

Ezzlie Somebody has screwed up big time! Phone? Phone?
Frances There! There on the table. I would ——
Ezzlie (*dialling*) Bastards!
Taxi Driver And what about my money?
Frances I'm sure she means to pay ——
Ezzlie (*shouting into the phone*) You bastard! You four-eyed snake! You stinking skunk! You cold conniving double crossing ... You knew! You told me a mansion at the edge of the city ... A little mansion you said! ... Well Little Frigging Mansion happens to be the name of the frigging little village! And The Little Mansion you lead me to believe would be my home is a frigging little semi at the end of a terrace! And you, you cheap-skate, you only bought me a one-way ticket! ... If it wasn't for me, you grasping-squint-eyed weasel-of-an-agent, you wouldn't have a pot to pish in ... How dare you sit there, behind your big antique desk, bought from my blood and sweat, and tell me you have bigger clients! Nobody! Nobody you had was bigger than me! Get up here! Get up here and get me out of this flaming nightmare ... What do you mean until I get on my feet? I wouldn't be off my feet if you had done your job right! I should never have trusted you! You're an agent for frig's sake, why did I trust you? ... You can't tear up my contract! I'll sue the dangling balls off you, you ferret-faced bast ... Hello! Hello!

She slams the phone down. Frances and the Taxi Driver just stare at her in disbelief

Taxi Driver And what about my money?
Ezzlie (*to Frances*) For Christ's sake give him his money!
Frances Yes! Yes of course. (*She fumbles with her bag*) Two twenties and a ten is that all right?
Taxidriver £49 on the clock, do you want the change?
Frances No. No.
Ezzlie (*shouting*) Giver her the frigging change!
Taxi Driver (*flipping a £1 coin towards her*) Here! Keep it for your swear box.

The Taxi Driver exits

*Frances quickly closes the door and they both stand staring at
each other*

Ezzlie And who are you?
Frances Frances.
Ezzlie (*after a pause*) Well? Is that all you have to say? Is there
    anything else?
Frances You look smaller on the telly.
Ezzlie And when did you last see me on "the telly"?
Frances Last night, or two a.m. this morning I stayed up to
    watch "Dancing In The Sun" ——
Ezzlie Well Frances, "Dancing In The Sun" was a mistake I
    made over thirty-five years ago. I would think even you were
    smaller thirty-five years ago *n'est ce* par?
Frances Yes. Oh yes. Did you say Nest café?
Ezzlie No, I said is there anything to drink in this place?
Frances Oh yes. I can make us some Earl Grey ——
Ezzlie I'm more of a Johnny Walker person. Look, Fran, I'm
    going to find the john upstairs. Why don't you see what you
    can do in the scotch department?
Frances I can show you around ——
Ezzlie Believe me, hun, I just know this place is going to be a
    two-up, two-down. I'll do the two-up, and you fix me some-
    thing in the two-down, something with ice and the smell of
    whisky ——
Frances I'm not much of a drinker ——
Ezzlie Really? Well I am. I am much of a drinker. And especially
    when I'm pissed off!

Ezzlie goes up the stairs

*Frances stands gaping. And then opens an old cocktail cabinet
and brings out odd miniatures. She pours bits from each miniature
into two glasses. She holds them until Ezzlie appears*

Ezzlie enters

Ezzlie Stinking pink everywhere!

Frances Your favourite colour right?

Ezzlie God help me! (*She pauses*) Are you just going to stand there with those drinks?

Frances Why don't you sit down, you are making me nervous.

Ezzlie If that's what it takes.

Frances I'm sorry about the ice. I didn't fill the ice tray in the fridge. I'll do it tomorrow ——

Ezzlie Oh God! There is still tomorrow.

Frances The big room is for you ——

Ezzlie Yeah, yeah, and for the few days that I might have to stay. I'll use that little room as a dressing-room. (*She drinks*)

Frances But that's my roo ——

Ezzlie (*blurting out the drink*) What the hell is in that?

Frances Everything I had.

Ezzlie When you fill the ice trays tomorrow, make sure you bring a bottle of Johnnie Walker, Black Label. You come every day do you?

Frances I live here.

Ezzlie What? For Christ's sake! I thought you were the cleaner!

Frances This is my house, my home.

Ezzlie So it was you who leased it to my agent.

Frances I invited you to stay as a guest in my house, (*beat*) with me, together, (*beat*) as friends.

Ezzlie Who the fuck are you?

Frances I am going to have to ask you to stop swearing at me. You are making me very nervous ——

Ezzlie Not half as nervous as I am right now! (*She swigs her drink*)

Frances It said on the telly you were penniless and homeless, and I just wanted to help you. So I wrote to you, care of your agent.

Ezzlie And that bastard! With his eight-bedroom house, shipped me out without a second glance.

Frances Are you?

Ezzlie What? Am I what? (*She throws back the drink*) I'm going to need another drink. Is there more of that concoction you brewed?

Frances passes her own untouched glass to Ezzlie

I'll stay one day until I sort this mess out.

Frances Is it true? Are you homeless?

Ezzlie Five star hotels are my home.

Frances They're very expensive.

Ezzlie Only if you pay.

Frances I read they are going sue you for thousands.

Ezzlie Well they can get in line, right behind the taxman and a few disgruntled producers. Suing Ezzlie Harlow seems to be a national pastime. I've made a lot of people rich, including three ex husbands. Men! Go figure! Can't live with them can't fuc — I mean have sex without them. What are you blushing at? Are you married?

Frances No.

Ezzlie Never?

Frances No.

Ezzlie Never had a man?

Frances No. Yes. I mean I've never been married.

Ezzlie Been around the block though?

Frances I'm sorry! I find this very personal.

Ezzlie You find this very personal? Saint fricking Frances of Hicksville finds this personal. Fran the Fan finds this personal. You know what I find personal, Fran? Have you any idea what I find personal? Go on, ask me! Ask me what I find personal!

Frances I don't know ——

Ezzlie I said ask me! Ask me what I find personal!

Frances What?

Ezzlie That you would dare to invite me, ME! To live with you! That you, with your no-life existence dared to intrude into my life; I find that personal. I find it personal that you had the affrontery to think a star of my stature would even acknowledge your existence. You with your cheap pen, and your cheap notepaper, and your cheap sentiments, getting me in to this fix. That's what I find personal.

Frances You didn't have to accept.

Ezzlie I didn't accept! Do you think I read all the drivel that crackpot fans write? My agent accepted. You gave him the perfect opportunity to get rid of me. How personal can you get? I was doing just fine shacked up in that bastard's guest house, making him pay for all the money he's leeched out of me.

Frances The papers said you were destitute ——

Ezzlie Oh please! The papers will say anything.

Frances Then everything is all right with you? You don't need me? I'm very sorry I interfered.

Ezzlie You're sorry?

Frances It's just that over the years your singing has brought so much pleasure ...You always seemed so sincere ... There were times when all I had to do was listen to your voice, and I swear the sun would come out ... Your songs have such a deep understanding of life ... Many years ago, I came to see you on stage, in London. You were like a goddess, you glistened, and we in the audience were your slaves. When you sang, you laughed, you cried, and you made me feel all your joy and all of your pain. I waited at the stage door just to say hello, and when you came out you signed my programme. You asked my name, and then you wrote, "Frances, follow your dream". Your next big hit was "Follow Your Dream", and somehow I thought that song was about me, from you to me ...There isn't a day goes by that I don't think about you, I am so grateful to you, you brought me through some very dark times. So I am more than sorry if I have done anything that could jeopardize your position with your agent. I just wanted you to know you had a fan who cared ...

Very long pause

Should I take your suitcase upstairs?

Ezzlie Yeah.

Frances leaves with the suitcase

Ezzlie quietly looks around the shabby sitting-room

Dear God in heaven, please deliver me from the kindness of strangers.

The Lights fade

SCENE 2

The same. Five days later

The Lights come up on Frances, in an old shabby flannelette nightgown, in a made-up bed on the sofa. She is writing in her diary

Frances It's five days now. Says she will be leaving soon, but her agent won't accept her calls, and his secretary said he had packed up all her belongings for forwarding. She won't leave the house, says she's frightened of being recognized. But quite honestly without her make-up and costumes she looks almost normal. Sometimes even I forget how great she was; I mean is, is. It doesn't seem to bother her that she has a cash flow problem. I suppose when you are used to great wealth you forget how to economize. I have to keep the ice tray filled for ice. She likes ice ... mostly in her whisky. Mr Patel, my lovely grocer, was quite surprised when I asked him for another bottle of Johnnie Walker Black Label; he gave me a rather flirtatious look, which made me feel quite sophisticated, so I put a tin of black olives in the basket, just to show him it's not always pork pies for tea. I wonder if he likes me. It is all strangely exciting having her here.

The Lights fade

SCENE 3

The same

The Lights come up

Ezzlie enters the sitting-room in a flowing silk dressing gown

Frances is off in the small kitchen. They call to each other

Ezzlie Coffee!
Frances (*off*) It's ready!
Ezzlie Black!
Frances (*off*) I know!
Ezzlie And close that goddam window! I smell autumn in the air! I hate autumn! The fall; rotting leaves.
Frances (*off*) I'm just preparing lunch.
Ezzlie And what delights have I got to look forward to today? What excruciating culinary delights are you cooking up today?
Frances (*off*) It's Friday, I usually have fish on a Friday ——
Ezzlie Smoked salmon would be nice ——

Frances enters with the coffee

Frances It's kippers. I wouldn't know how to cook smoked salmon.
Ezzlie I don't think you know how to cook anything!
Frances We could go out for a meal ——
Ezzlie A meal? You mean real food?
Frances If you don't like what I serve here, we could go out one night.
Ezzlie How much money have you got?
Frances In my purse?

Ezzlie In the bank?

Frances Only what my mother left.

Ezzlie You didn't earn your own money?

Frances I had to take care of Mother all of my adult life ——

Ezzlie God help her!

Frances It wasn't easy. She was a very difficult woman.

Ezzlie So you have a good size nest egg?

Frances If I'm careful there's enough to see me into old age ——

Ezzlie You are in old age.

Frances I'm only fifty-five, and I don't spend a lot.

Ezzlie You look sixty-eight! Why have you let your hair go grey?

Frances I couldn't stop it.

Ezzlie What a mess you are!

Frances I have a home and a few thousand pounds in the bank. If you have more than that you don't need to be here.

Ezzlie I have what you will never have. I have a TALENT!

Frances Then use it. Save your own life.

Ezzlie What do you know about life? Have you ever been in love? Have you ever had your heart broken over and over again by a man you worship and adore? Have you made love in a limo, or on a beach at midnight? Have you ever tied a big red bow on a Maserati and given it to a Greek god just because he said he loved you? I've been used and abused. And I've used and abused right back! I've been dumped and I have dumped. The only difference being, when I dumped them it cost me millions of bucks; when they dumped me I got zilch! I've watched my fortune dwindle and rekindle, money has never worried me; I have always been able to sing for my supper. What have you ever done?

Frances Nothing, nothing at all. And yet here you are, standing in my front room sharing all of this with me. What did I do to deserve that? Excuse me while I fill the ice tray.

Frances storms off

Ezzlie (*calling after her*) And do you think we could have more than six ice cubes at a time?
Frances (*off*) I only have one ice tray!
Ezzlie   Use your inheritance and buy another! Live dangerously.

The Lights fade

SCENE 4

The same

The Lights come up on Frances in her sofa-bed. She is dressed in a flimsy silk nightdress, writing her diary. Tall cardboard boxes litter the room with feather boas and glittering costumes hanging over some of them

Frances   Dear Diary, Ezzlie has been here over four weeks, and she is very depressed; her agent has sold off a lot of her stuff to settle some of her debts. He has informed the newspapers that Ezzlie Harlow has retired to Mexico. The rest of her belongings he has sent here. She doesn't want anyone to know her predicament, so, she has to go along with the agent's story about Mexico. She's been quite melancholy, but she did kindly give me this silk nightie. She said seeing me in Mam's old nighties is more than she could bear. I had never felt silk all over my body before, it's quite a nice sensation, and what dreams it gives me. I dreamed I walked in to Mr Patel's shop wearing only this ... Sadly I woke up before he noticed me! All of Ezzlie's beautiful stage gowns are here in my front room. I have never seen so many feathers, sequins and fur! I hope she can shake off her depression. I bought her some smoked salmon to try and cheer her up, it seems you don't have to cook it; it's not to my taste at all, but she seems to like it. However, you should have seen Mr Patel's face when I walked in there wearing the little mink jacket; Ezzlie made me put it on, said she couldn't stand the sight of me in my mam's old raincoat. Well, Mr Patel was almost attentive, he ordered in the smoked salmon special, and told me I should have a delivery as carrying all the bottles could be a strain; even suggested I should open an account with him, which Ezzlie thinks is a brilliant idea. But, but, oh dear I'm getting strange butterfly feelings about Mr P, and thoughts, strange exciting thoughts. I wonder if he ever thinks of me? (*Writing*) Of course he doesn't! Oh dear Diary, now you know all my secrets ——

The door bursts open

Ezzlie stands dressed in a white satin feather-trimmed dressing gown; an empty glass in her hand

Ezzlie So this is what you get up to in the wee hours! What you gonna do, sell my story to the papers and become a minor celebrity!

Frances No!

Ezzlie Well, what's that you're writing? Tomorrow's grocery list for the handsome Mr Patel?

Frances Can I get you something?

Ezzlie Yeah! I've used up my six ice cubes.

Frances I'm defrosting the fridge. I didn't think you would need ice in the middle of the night.

Ezzlie How do you think I get through the night?

Frances You've had no fresh air since you got here ——

Ezzlie I told you I hate autumn, who wants to see all those faded falling leaves? That's what was best about LA: no seasons, and ice at the press of a button.

Frances There must be more to LA than that ——

Ezzlie No. That's it. Just that. No fall, and lots, and lots of ice.

Frances You must have made many famous friends there.

Ezzlie No. But I made many famous enemies. Anyway, who needs friends when you have hairdressers, make-up artists, designers and PRs scurrying around, and all on the pay roll?

Frances You don't need all those people just to sing. We would love you if you sang in a sack.

Ezzlie No you wouldn't, you just so would not. Ordinary people come to watch extraordinary people perform, and without all of the razzle and dazzle I'm just plain ordinary. All of my oomph and confidence came from the rhinestones and feathers contained there in all of those boxes. That's what you came to see.

Frances I think you underestimate the public. I'll make you some tea ——

Ezzlie My agent has deserted me. My record company has dropped me, and producers find Ezzlie Harlow too difficult to work with. Strange thing is, there is no Ezzlie Harlow. Ezzlie Harlow was manufactured by agents, record companies, and producers.

Frances Then who is this feeling sorry for herself?

Ezzlie Good question. Tonight folks, I'm little me. Elsie Barrow, born in Sheffield.

Frances But you're American, born in the USA ——

Ezzlie Says who? My stage-struck mother took me to California when I was a kid. She wanted to further her own pitiful career, but somewhere along the way I became the breadwinner. They gave me a new identity, but I still remember the little terrace house we left behind. Two-up and two-down. So here I am right back where I started.

Frances What are you going to do about it?

Ezzlie Die. Can you think of anything else?

Frances Dying can take quite a while; it took my mother years. I can't afford to keep you that long.

Ezzlie Tough! You wanted me, you got me! If your cooking doesn't kill me, maybe a few of those sleeping pills you've got stashed in the bathroom can help.

Frances They don't work.

Ezzlie Oh, have been there have we?

Pause

Frances What about all this stuff?

Ezzlie You can sell the costumes to pay for my funeral.

Frances I could try and sell one to the man who impersonates you, that would keep you in whisky for another few months ——

Ezzlie What man impersonates me?

Frances He's very good ——

Ezzlie A man does me?

Frances Mostly you, some Shirley Bassey, and Dusty Spring-field ——

Ezzlie A man?

Frances You know, a lady man.

Ezzlie A drag queen?

Frances He's very glamorous. He would be better if he had the right costumes. He fills the place.

Ezzlie What place?

Frances fishes out the local paper from under the sofa and gives it to Ezzlie

Frances Here! Look in the paper, there's his ad.

Ezzlie (*reading*) "Danny Define, Carlisle, Penrith, Kendal, Lancaster, Morecambe", he's got a whole fricking tour going, and he doesn't look anything like me!

Frances He looks more like you, than you look like you. Of course he doesn't have your voice.

Ezzlie Of course he doesn't have my voice.

Frances A lot of people would come to see someone with your voice.

Ezzlie No one has my voice.

Frances Elsie Barrow has your voice.

Ezzlie That's all Elsie Barrow has got.

Frances Maybe she should start singing for her supper.

Ezzlie Maybe dying is a better career move!

Frances If he can impersonate you, why can't you imperson-ate you?

Ezzlie He earns nickels and dimes.

Frances That's more than you're earning right now.

Ezzlie Who are you, my agent all of a sudden? Little Miss No-Life-Franny. Oh Fran the Fan has had a whiff of the big time and wants to hitch her wagon to a star. Failure Fran never had a man ——

Frances slaps Ezzlie across the face

Frances You ungrateful bitch!
Ezzlie How dare you!
Frances I'm sorry but somebody should have done that a long time ago.
Ezzlie Who the hell do you think you are?
Frances I know who I am. But who do you think you *still* are? You have NO agent. You have NO recording contract. And you have NO army of people to get you on stage. All you have at this moment is ME.
Ezzlie And that's why I want to die! Ezzlie Harlow is no more! Sell her costumes to Danny Define and bury her in a little black dress.
Frances Is that what you really want?
Ezzlie All I ever wanted was to be like Piaf. But the big boys didn't "get" the little black dress. They wanted the glitz, the sizzle, the whole razzle-dazzle and they built an industry around me; I was their big shimmering logo. And then they pulled the plug.
Frances I think you pulled the plug.
Ezzlie Whatever. Where's that drink you were going to get?
Frances I can get you something better than that.

Frances exits

Ezzlie picks up the paper and reads the ad

Ezzlie "Where are they now? Watch Danny Define bring to life the stars of yesteryear. You've seen the rest now see the best". Yesteryear? Where are they now? Bring to life? Who does this guy think he is? I'm still here goddamyou! I'm still here, aren't I? Aren't I? (*Beat*) Or am I there, there in those boxes? Yes there I am, that's me, all sequins, tassels and tinsel, tassels and tinsel; tinsel that's me.

Frances enters carrying a wire coathanger with a little black dress hanging from it

I hate this guy! Who does he think he is? Yesteryear, where are they now? When they ask that about me, they'll find me here, rotting like fallen leaves, "Ezzlie Harlow died in the last house in the last street in the last place on earth" if I wasn't dead I'd die of shame ——

Frances You're dying from fame not shame.

Ezzlie I need a drink! What's that?

Frances It's the little black dress.

Ezzlie Whose is it?

Frances Well Ezzlie Harlow could be buried in it, or Elsie Barrow could start a new career in it. A simple ordinary career, doing what she does best, singing.

Ezzlie Singing what? The minute I sing one of my hits they would know ——

Frances There's plenty of un-sung, un-hit songs ——

Ezzlie Like the blues, (*she hums a bar of the blues*) or jazz maybe? (*She scats a few bars of jazz*)

Frances Yes! But with no glitter, no feathers, no sequins, no ——

Ezzlie OK I get it!

Frances Just a simple ——

Ezzlie I'm getting it; a simple ordinary bread and butter career, singing for my supper.

Frances Nothing but a piano ——

Ezzlie And a spotlight, there'd have to be a spotlight, a spotlight on me in a little black dress.

Frances That's all you need, even I could organize that.

Ezzlie You? Have you ever organized anything in your whole life?

Frances Yes. I have! And it was very successful.
Ezzlie What?
Frances Mam's funeral. I pulled the whole thing together on my own, with just a telephone.
Ezzlie And that's what you're going to do for me is it?
Frances I could try. Your new career I mean, not your funeral!
Ezzlie Same thing. Why do I feel depressed?

Frances grabs her pen and diary

Frances It will pass! We'll make a list, I always feel better once I start making lists. Now! One?
Ezzlie The only lists you make are for your grocer man.
Frances This is for you. One?
Ezzlie A bottle of peroxide.
Frances (*writing*) Per-ox-ide. Two? (*Beat*) TWO?
Ezzlie OK! An ad in the trades for a pianist.
Frances (*writing*) Trade ad pianist. Three?

The Lights fade

SCENE 5

The same

The Lights come up on Frances who is standing, listening on the phone. She wears the same smart suit that Ezzlie arrived in and her hair is short and blond

Frances I'm glad you liked the demo. ... No. She doesn't mime ... She has her own pianist. ... It doesn't have to be a grand piano. An upright will be fine as long as you have it tuned. ... Elsie is her real name, no she doesn't want to change it. ... £250 for her and the pianist per performance? Could you stretch that to £300? I know you pay Danny Define more than that. ... She will please them, if she doesn't I'll return you £350. ... A tuned piano and a good spotlight that's her only requirements. Oh! By the way do you have plenty of ice?... Thank you. Don't worry, she'll be there, she is very professional. (*She puts the phone down, she looks in the mirror and shakes her hair*)

Ezzlie (*off, calling*) OK! Are you ready?

Frances I'm ready!

Ezzlie Well here comes ME!

Ezzlie enters wearing the little black dress and a short bobbed black wig. She makes a couple of twirls then sings a few verses of "Some Changes Made" (lyrics by Billy Higgins, music Benton Overstreet, published in 1921)

Frances (*clapping*) Look at you!

Ezzlie How ordinary do I look now?

Frances You could never look ordinary. You look special.

Ezzlie And you took my advice and dressed the part.

Frances Advice? You bullied me into this outfit.

Ezzlie The talented Mr Patel was quite smitten with your new peroxide hair ——

Frances He is talented, isn't he?

Ezzlie Was he really the only one to answer your ad?

Frances In a way, yes.

Ezzlie In a way? What do you mean, in a way? What way?

Frances I gave him the "rehearsal pianist wanted ad" to put in his shop window, and that's when he told me he plays the piano ——

Ezzlie Goddam, Fran! When I told you to advertise for a pianist in one of the trades, I didn't mean in a tradesman's shop window!

Frances Well, we got one didn't we? And he's as good as any, isn't he? He would have formed his own group, but his father made him take over the family business. He is good, isn't he?

Ezzlie He's good. Dammed good ——

Frances And he has his delivery van to get us there, that's a saving.

Ezzlie Thank God, with you as my manager, there's not a hope
  in hell's chance of me ever being famous again.
Frances Is that a good thing?
Ezzlie It's a great thing.

The doorbell rings

  There's our driver, pianist, grocer now.
Frances (*excited*) Here we go to our first jig ——
Ezzlie Gig, Frances, gig!

The Lights fade

SCENE 6

The same. A year later

*The Lights come up on Frances, smartly dressed, writing at her
desk. There is a recording of Ezzlie playing in the background*

Frances Dear Diary, It's been a bouncy year, lots of ups and
  downs, of course Elsie Barrow and Confry Patel have become
  well known on the club circuit; they are a talented double
  act called Simple Jazz. The local paper gave me the credit of
  discovering them. But the only time I discovered them was
  when they were in bed together. Ezzlie told me to get over it,
  she said: "That's showbusiness!" I still represent them, and
  also Danny Define. Danny Define is now quite famous with
  his impersonation of Ezzlie Harlow. He says he owes it all to
  me for finding him the original costumes. There has been talk
  in some papers that he really is Ezzlie Harlow. Confry and
  Elsie have moved into a new riverside flat not far from here,
  and his young brother, Mr Patel, runs the shop now. Ezzlie's
  old agent suspects something; he rang me to say he could get
  me a book deal if I wanted to sell my story. But I just told
  him there was no story, and that Ezzlie Harlow had left me

and gone to live in Mexico. I think even ten minutes of fame
would not suit me.

The doorbell rings and Frances opens it

Ezzlie stands there

Ezzlie How are we?
Frances I'm fine.
Ezzlie You're the finest, but how are we, you and me?
Frances (*after a pause*) Do you want to come in?
Ezzlie Do you want me to come in?
Frances Come in.
Ezzlie Are you busy?
Frances I'm busy turning down work in London for you, and
    TV offers ——
Ezzlie Great! Keep up the bad work. Got anything to drink?
Frances Some leftover Johnnie Walker there, but I haven't had
    time to fill the ice tray.
Ezzlie No need to ever fill another ice tray! (*Pouring two drinks*)
    Look out of the window.
Frances (*staring through the window*) My God what is that?
    That's the biggest red bow I have ever seen!
Ezzlie That baby is a genuine cellophane-gift-wrapped new
    sub-zero-refrigerator with a permanent icemaker at the press
    of a button.
Frances A new fridge. For me?
Ezzlie For you! (*She gives her a drink*)
Frances But you shouldn't waste your money on me.
Ezzlie Why not? I owe you a lot more ——
Frances You don't owe me anything.
Ezzlie Would you believe me if I told you, in all my years in show-
    biz you are the most interesting woman I have ever met?
Frances No.
Ezzlie Good. That's good. It proves you're not as gullible as you
    once were. But truly, you are the only person I trust.
Frances I wish I could say the same.

Ezzlie Can't you forgive me?
Frances For what? Shattering my delusion?
Ezzlie Look at you! You're a stylish woman. Once you get the hang of it, you'll be breaking a few men's hearts, because, you like me, are a S O B ——
Frances Meaning what?
Ezzlie We're Sexy-Old-Birds.
Frances Elsie Barrow you are still so shameless!!
Ezzlie I know. But please let me be your friend.
Frances To think, that's all I really ever wanted.
Ezzlie That proves it then!
Frances Proves what?
Ezzlie That we have to be careful of the things we really want, because sometimes we get them.
Frances Is that showbusiness?
Ezzlie No, that's life! Cheers.

They lift their glasses and toast each other

Frances To life then!

Optional ending: both singing "Changes Made"

THE END

FURNITURE AND PROPERTY LIST

SCENE 1

On stage: Sofa. *On it*: pink cushions
Cocktail cabinet. *In it*: various miniatures, glasses
Table. *On it*: pen, **Frances'** diary, telephone
Mirror on wall
Frances' handbag containing purse with notes and £1
    coins

Off stage: Heavy suitcase (**Taxi Driver**)

SCENE 2

Set: Blanket and pillows on sofa

SCENE 3

Strike: Blanket and pillows from sofa

Off stage: Tray of coffee (**Frances**)

SCENE 4

Strike: Tray of coffee

Set: Blanket and pillows on sofa
Tall cardboard boxes, overflowing with feather boas,
    glittering costumes
Local paper under sofa

Off stage: Empty glass (**Ezzlie**)
                   Little black dress on wire coat hanger (**Frances**)

SCENE 5

Strike: Blanket and pillows from sofa
                   Cardboard boxes and contents
                   Little black dress on wire coathanger
                   Blanket and pillows from

SCENE 6

Set: Near empty bottle of whisky and two glasses on the
                   cocktail cabinet

LIGHTING PLOT

Property fittings required: nil
Interior, the same scene throughout

SCENE 1

To open: General interior lighting

Cue 1   **Ezzlie**: " ... the kindness of strangers."   (Page 8)
           Fade to black-out

SCENE 2

To open: General interior lighting

Cue 2   **Frances**: " ... strangely exciting having her here.   (Page 8)
           Fade to black-out

SCENE 3

To open: General interior lighting

Cue 3   **Ezzlie**: "Live dangerously."   (Page 11)
           Fade to black-out

SCENE 4

To open: Dimmer interior lighting

Cue 4   **Frances**: "Trade ad pianist. Three?"   (Page 17)
           Fade to black-out

SCENE 5

To open: General interior lighting

Cue 5   **Ezzlie**: "Gig, Frances, gig!   (Page 19)
           Fade to black-out

SCENE 6

To open: General interior lighting

No cues

EFFECTS PLOT

Cue 1   **Frances**: " ... going to be my friend."   (Page 2)
            Doorbell

Cue 2   **Ezzlie**: "It's a great thing."   (Page 19)
            Doorbell rings

Cue 3   To open SCENE 6   (Page 19)
            Recording of **Ezzlie** *plays in the background. Fade*
                as **Frances** *speaks*

Cue 4   **Frances**: " ... would not suit me."   (Page 20)
            Doorbell